FISH HAPPENS

WORDS OF WISDOM
FROM THE PENGUINS

F/SH HAPPENS

WORDS OF WISDOM
FROM THE PENGUINS

by Brian Elling

Grosset & Dunlap
An Imprint of Penguin Group (USA) Inc.

GROSSET & DUNLAP
Published by the Penguin Group
Penguin Group (USA) Inc., 375 Hudson Street, New York, New York 10014, USA
Penguin Group (Canada), 90 Eglinton Avenue East, Suite
700, Toronto, Ontario M4P 2Y3, Canada
(a division of Pearson Penguin Canada Inc.)
Penguin Books Ltd., 80 Strand, London WC2R 0RL, England
Penguin Group Ireland, 25 St. Stephen's Green, Dublin 2, Ireland
(a division of Penguin Books Ltd.)
Penguin Group (Australia), 250 Camberwell Road, Camberwell, Victoria 3124, Australia
(a division of Pearson Australia Group Pty. Ltd.)
Penguin Books India Pvt. Ltd., 11 Community Centre,
Panchsheel Park, New Delhi—110 017, India
Penguin Group (NZ), 67 Apollo Drive, Rosedale, Auckland 0632, New Zealand
(a division of Pearson New Zealand Ltd.)
Penguin Books (South Africa) (Pty.) Ltd., 24 Sturdee Avenue,
Rosebank, Johannesburg 2196, South Africa

Penguin Books Ltd., Registered Offices: 80 Strand, London WC2R 0RL, England

ISBN 978-0-448-49552-1   10 9 8 7 6 5 4 3 2 1

Dear Human,

Do you smell that? That slimy, sour feeling that's been following you around for days? You know what that is? **FISH.** It happens.

No matter who you are, *what* you are, or even if you're not evolved enough to know what you are, sometimes things in this world just don't go exactly as planned. What can I say? It's just the **nature** of . . . nature.

So my elite penguin force and I find it only natural that lesser creatures like yourselves (no need to be ashamed) need a little help from the species with the greatest evolutionary success. The species that put the **WIN** in *Darwin.* The species that slid belly-first to the very apex of biological development.

PENGUINS.

No matter where your problems fall on the range of our patented Penguin Problem-o-Meter, we have a solution for you.

SMALL
PROBLEM

P   R   O   B   L   E   M

Power Outage   Banana Peel on Sidewalk

BIG PROBLEM

O - M E T E R

Giant Meteor

Any Problem That's Your Fault

7

SKIPPER

I'm Skipper. I am the leader of the penguin force. My job is to lead my team through each mission with **bravado**, **conviction**, and **confidence**. And even when I get it wrong . . . well, **I'm still more right than you**. That's why you're reading this book. (I've seen who you've put in Congress . . . Trust me, you need us!)

Rico is our demolitions expert. He **uses his GUT**
to solve problems (literally—he stores an arsenal in
his stomach). You can always count on this guy to
blow up or demolish anything that gets in his way.
This is a very effective way to solve your problems if
you're capable of working with explosives and have
the ability to think quickly under pressure.*

*HUMANS: PLEASE SEEK GREATER SPECIES
SUPERVISION BEFORE EXPLODING THINGS AT HOME.

KOWALSKI

Kowalski is the **brains** of the operation. He can ponder potential solutions to a problem long before there's a problem to solve. Why, I'd bet my fresh fish that **he could achieve world peace**, cure all incurable diseases, and create a sustainable development system to preserve life on Earth for another millennium **in the time it takes you to wash behind your ears**. **What?! You've *never* done that?** Well . . . no wonder the world is such a mess.

PRIVATE

And last, but certainly not least, here's Private. This guy is all **heart**. He lets his emotions guide him through life. No matter the situation, Private wears his heart on his flippers, and he knows how to **solve any problem** using a little kindness. Except when it comes to **unicorns or candy**. But give the guy a break! You humans are swayed by far more destructive and addictive things. Like golf. And shoes. Who needs 'em?

So you see? This elite penguin force is fully equipped to guide you through any problem.

And for those really hard cases, we've employed the help of some friends from the zoo.

WHEN THINGS GET
FISHY

As soon as you encounter a particularly fishy problem, it's best to handle the situation **immediately**.

By handling a crisis when it first occurs, you are more likely to contain the problem, minimizing resulting damage. Most importantly, you will be certain that **no one else finds out**.

Chapter 1

ZEN and the ART OF ANXIETY

When a problem occurs, it's important to remain **calm**. Of course, the best way to stay cool is to not have a problem happen in the first place. This can be achieved through proper planning, communication, and common sense. But when these techniques fail (and they often do), you may experience **anxiety**.

Anxiety is that queasy feeling in the pit of your stomach that tells you something's not right. It kind of feels like **indigestion**—only without the fun of eating too much first.

Anxiety can also cause a throbbing headache, like when you've been captured and hung upside down for too long (which can be very anxiety-producing in itself . . .

DOUBLE HEADACHE!).

If you've got anxiety about a problem you can't solve, try sleeping on it. Most problems seem a lot less terrible after a **good night's sleep**.

Especially if you've had hot cocoa before bed and dream about bunnies eating lollipops like Private does. He always gets a good night's rest.

If sleeping doesn't work and you find yourself startled awake with worry, **DON'T PANIC**. You've got options to manage your anxiety.

Try distracting yourself by watching TV. If you watch crime dramas, family dramas, and soap operas regularly, you can remind yourself that most of life's problems are **ridiculous**. And the rest are **solvable**, usually within a half hour.

Don't blow your problems out of proportion. For example, that giant alligator behind you may not want to **eat** you at all. He may just want to share a plate of **freshly baked cookies**. Who knows? It could happen.

And **believing in yourself** is a great way to minimize anxiety. Trust that you'll figure everything out in your own time.

After all, just because you've wiped out on that latest skateboard trick eighteen times doesn't mean you won't stick the landing on the next try! And if you still don't . . . well, at least you're learning a lot about how to fall down.

Another way to avoid anxiety is to remember that things could always be **worse**. For example, you could be trapped in the lair of an evil dolphin who's out to destroy the world.

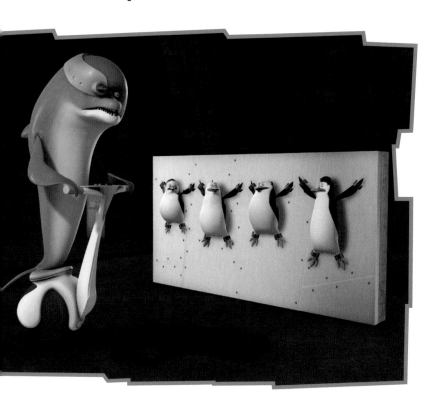

Thinking about worst-case scenarios is a great way to remind yourself how **lucky** you are to have the problems you have.

And don't forget, sometimes your problem will be resolved through nothing more than dumb luck!

In cases like these, you can put that anxious energy to better use. Like enjoying the rare feeling of having good luck.

Aces!

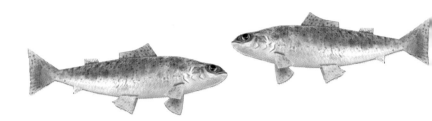

You'll feel less anxious once you realize that you're never alone. **Everyone** has **problems** and **anxiety.** Especially humans. They spend a good part of each day wondering, *what can* **POSSIBLY** *happen to me* ***next***?

By avoiding anxiety, you'll be more relaxed and better prepared to handle whatever problems come your way. This will make you as calm and happy as a **PENGUIN.**

Chapter 2

MARLENE'S GUIDE TO

SOLVING
Your PROBLEMS

Hi! I'm Marlene. Skipper didn't officially introduce me because I'm not part of the elite penguin force. No, it's not because I'm an **otter**. (You thought I was going to say *girl*, didn't you?) It's because I'm an **expert** at just about everything . . . that's why the Penguins keep me in the loop. I'm **the *otter* penguin**.

What most creatures of little brainpower don't realize is that most of life's problems will resolve themselves spontaneously if totally ignored. Cover your eyes, ears, and mouth, or simply turn around, and *poof!* PROBLEM GONE. Like it never happened.

But sometimes problems occur that can't be ignored. These problems can be classified as:

Something **Humans** Will Notice (this means they're a *BIG deal*—a lot gets by you guys)

OR

Something Your **Friends** Will Notice (this means the problem does not fit under the bed)

In either of these cases, you'll need to **take action** to hide the problem. An elaborate distraction technique is often effective. Like a

FAN DANCE!

A little **color** always makes a crime scene look less crime-y—even for the fishiest, messiest crime scene imaginable. Like when I stole all the Penguins' fish. A **pink flamingo** kept those Penguins away from the scene like a scarecrow keeps kids out of a cornfield. The *otter* penguin is a **genius**.

No matter how you **hide** your problem, you'll want to make sure there is **no possible way** for it to be **discovered** accidentally.

For problems that are **too big** to be shoved in the back of a closet, you can hide them in plain sight by simply denying their existence. Saying "I never said that!" or "What angry rhinoceros?" is often enough to convince others that there's not a problem to begin with.

However, in extreme cases, you may need to employ the help of a **friend*** to assist you in hiding a problem. These friends can be called *accomplices*.

When choosing which of your friends would make the best accomplice, it's helpful to select someone who's trying to hide a problem of their own. Knowing your **friends' secrets** is the best way to be sure they won't **rat*** you out.

*NO OFFENSE INTENDED TO ACTUAL RODENTS.

If you don't happen to have any dirt on your friends to keep them quiet, offering them gifts is a good way to ensure they won't reveal your secret. Sometimes this is called **bribery**. Sometimes it's called *convincing your friend to help you solve a problem with a little incentive*. You can use whichever definition you feel more comfortable with.

Whether you offer an incentive or not, you should always make sure your accomplice can **follow your instructions**. After all, it's **your problem**, so they should solve it your way. (If they actually knew better than you do, they wouldn't have let you get into the problem in the first place.)

It's a lot of work to solve a problem, isn't it? Of course, you could just aspire to be **perfect** like me and then not have to worry about problems.

Ha! And you thought **solving** problems was hard . . .

Chapter 3

FINGERS—
POINT 'EM
IF YOU GOT 'EM

Kowalski here. And I'm perfectly pleased to tell you that the results are in.

As head of the FDA (Fowl Drug Administration), I've recently concluded extensive research on topical problem-resolution formulas and their success rates in the treatment of persistent **guilt** and **responsibility**.

According to my calculations, **BLAME**™ is the most overwhelmingly successful method of reducing or eradicating your own symptoms of guilt.*

*BASED ON A SAMPLE OF THREE LEMURS PLACED UNDER MODERATE GUILT DURING A TEN-WEEK PERIOD AS CONDUCTED BY KOWALSKI, PENGUIN GENIUS, NEW YORK ZOO LABS, 2012.

Before treating your guilt and responsibility, it's important to get an accurate diagnosis. Symptoms of guilt include:

1 **Knowing** you did something wrong

2 The feeling that **others** will **find out** you did something wrong

3 Persistent nail biting (because you've done something wrong)

But now there's a cure!

BLAME™ was found to be sixteen times more potent than any other remedy in my study.

6.3% Pretend No One Noticed

0.1% Apologize

93.6%
BLAME™

When using **BLAME**™, it's important to administer the treatment correctly. Otherwise **BLAME**™ may not work.

My deductive and inductive studies indicate that **BLAME**™ is most effective when placed on a member of the sample group who is "not quick on their feet" (3%), "not well-liked" (10.7%), or "furry" (86.3%).

Once you've decided who will
make you feel better, it's time to
take action. **BLAME**™ is quite
powerful; usually a simple
finger-pointing will do.

42

You'll know **BLAME**™ has worked when the person you blamed expresses the symptoms you were experiencing. (Refer to page 39.)

In addition to the traditional symptoms of guilt, the target will also show signs of **extreme disappointment** in themselves.

However, if for some reason the initial dose of **BLAME**™ isn't effective, you can incite an **angry mob** to deliver manual shots of **BLAME**™ until the target exhibits the symptoms described on page 39.

Treatment Report Summary for **BLAME**™ (generic: Noresponsibilityforyouractionsazine):

As you can see from the preceding evidence, **BLAME**™ has been proven to be an effective treatment for chronic guilt in zoo animals. When used consistently and in the correct manner, it can radically reduce symptoms of guilt, embarrassment, and/or sense of personal responsibility in the patient.

POSSIBLE SIDE EFFECTS OF **BLAME**™ INCLUDE HEADACHE, NAUSEA, PARANOIA, LOSS OF FRIENDS, LOW SELF-ESTEEM, WRATH OF A DEITY, AND EXTREMELY BAD KARMA.

Chapter 4

OPEN, HONEST, and ARCTIC-CULATE

Loose lips sink **ZOOS**, boys!

We Penguins know that when the worst happens, keeping it a **secret** might just save your life.

Rico knows more about secret-keeping than any other animal I know. Every time he opens his mouth, I expect one of those secrets to be let loose. But all he ever says is,

"BAWWWWWWWKKKKKKKKKK!"

Rico knows what even we Penguins sometimes forget: Honesty can be like dropping a **BOMB** on your friends and family.

That's right: The **truth** is **UGLY**. And once the truth is out there, you can't take it back. Just like a real bomb, the Honesty Bomb can leave devastating results.

So before you decide to drop the H-Bomb on someone, take a lesson from Rico and
keep your secrets to yourself.

Keeping secrets deep inside is not only good for you but is the best thing for your family and friends. No matter how much they pry, **don't give in**!

keep those secrets to yourself.

Chapter 5

How to **WIN** FRIENDS and INFLUENCE MINIONS

All hail me! King Julien!

As a **king**, I don't have all this time to be solving problems.

No one realizes how difficultish it is to be royalty. Seriously. Every day there's so much doing to do. There's the sitting. The eating. The more sitting in a different way. Not to mention how heavy the **crowns** are!

It's exhausting. *NO KING COULD DO it alone.*
That's why I have minions.

But how do you—a not royal kingly king—be
getting someone else to be dealing with all the
bad things so you can focus on your boogying?

First, establish yourself as **more importanter** than everyone else around you. Otherwise your minions won't realize they're minions.

Then sit back and be basking in your kinglyness while your minions solve your problems. **Never try to do anything.** It will make others think you are capable of doing things by yourself.

Second rule #2:

Be regularly **demanding** your minions to do things that are hard. Like finding you a magic carpet. This way, when you ask them to solve an easy problem, they will be overjoyed to fulfill your wishes.

Third rule #2:

Don't be forgetting to make your minions **compete to be your favorite**. For example, on the day that is not your birthday but you want to eat your birthday cake, tell one minion that another one is better at making your cake. This is a sure way to get them to try their hardest to please you.

(And for you to get many, many **DELICIOUS CAKES**.)

Fourth rule #2:

Play stupid! Be telling your minions that you really *want* to fix problems using your by-yourselfness. Then let them watch how **BaD** you are at it.

This way, next time they'll be eager to handle the crisis by their selfness, and you don't have to do anything.

And lastly, **YELL!**
Yelling is the bestest way to get a minion to do something for you. It inspires them to do more things for you until you're quiet again.

If you are following these rules very exactly, you can count on those around you having the energy to solve all your problems so you don't have to lift a kingly finger.

Unless you want to eat a banana by yourselfness. But if you are following my most royalest advice, you won't be needing to do anything by yourselfness again!

SECTION II:

AFTER FISH HAPPENS:

THE CLEANUP

If you can't hide from, ignore, or prevent bad things happening, there's only one option left: **solving** the problem. That's right. It's a smelly, rotten job, but someone's gotta do it. And since you got yourself into the mess, who better to get **you** out?

Chapter 6

Private's Guide to
OVERCOMING ADVERSITY:
The IMPORTANCE
of Being CUTE

When fish gets you down, the first thing you need to do is make sure you look your best. Dust off your flippers, **lift your beak** high, and smile like there's nothing wrong in the world.

To make this point absolutely clear, we've asked Private to pose for some "before" and "after" photos. Here's Private "before" fish happens:

BEFORE

And **AFTER**

What a transformation!

Penguins are **masters** of looking **cute**. And you can be, too!

Of course, when it comes to upping your cute
quotient, **dressing right** is of the utmost importance.

Tuxedos are appropriate for any occasion. After all,
the **clothes make the bird**!

Never underdress.

This may make you appear less cute, and then you'll be **blamed** for something you did.

To be truly cute, you must master the **penguin swagger**. Try to match that *awwwww*-inspiring waddle.

You'll also want to develop a full routine of cute antics to distract those around you when fish happens.

Like synchronized **swimming** routines.

Eighteenth-century **dance moves** like the minuet! Always cute and classy!

And the all-important group **tail shake**!

You'll know you've perfected your own personal cuteness when you get a standing ovation for **just being you**!

If you follow these simple steps to achieve optimum cuteness, when fish gets you down you won't even care. And not just because you look great, but because you'll be **so cuddly** that everyone will forget what you did wrong in the first place.

Who knows? Maybe you'll even make the cover of the New York Zoo brochure like Private. Talk about

cuuuute.

Chapter 7

A ROYAL PAIN:
How to Live with the KING IN YOUR Life

Hello. It's Maurice. Life is a royal **pain** in the **ringtail**, ain't it? Especially when that royal pain in the ringtail is your royal **boss**!

Bosses. Royal or not, we've all got them, even if they're just a parent. But it's how you deal with bosses that makes the fish **foul** or **grade-A sushi**.

To stay out of trouble, you gotta know when to do your job and **do it well**. Usually this is when the boss is watching.

When the boss *isn't* watching, that's when you can **have a little fun**.

And if your work isn't done by the end of the day, just **blame** it on your coworkers. That's what they're there for.

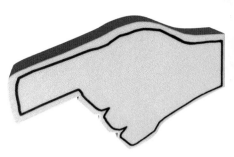

The thing about bosses is that they always think they know better than you do. So you've got to pretend to be totally supportive of all your boss's ideas . . .

. . . even though you have way better ones!

You've got to **save him from** himself . . .

. . . almost **daily**.

And then **give him all the credit**.

In other words, make your boss
feel special.

Even if it means giving him a
gift during the holidays.

Sometimes you've even got to carry the boss on your back! Literally and figuratively. Bosses don't get to the **top** without *a little* **boost** from their underlings.

And even though **you deserve** all the credit, don't ever let your boss know you dream of someday being in charge. It's good to have goals; you just can't ever let the boss know.

'Cause if you did, the boss might muster all his self-involved insecurities and **put you in your place**. Below him if you're lucky, on the street if you're not. And then you'd lose your health insurance and all that paid vacation.

I know it gets you down. Believe me, I'm exhausted by the end of the day, and I have to just get up and do it again the next day.

The trick is to never let him see you cry. And to not lose your will to live.

It's *just* a job.

He's just a lemur.

And you could take him in a fight.

All right, **Back to work!**

Chapter 8

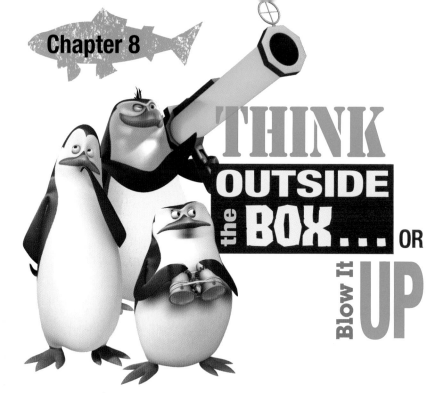

THINK OUTSIDE the BOX... OR Blow It UP

When you need to solve a really fishy problem, it's best to use brute force right away.

Don't waste time with diplomacy or negotiation when the simplest solution is to

BLOW it UP.*

*HUMANS: AGAIN, DO NOT HANDLE WEAPONS OR EXPLOSIVES WITHOUT A TRAINED PENGUIN EXPERT. YOU ARE NOT SMART ENOUGH TO DO THIS ON YOUR OWN. DON'T BELIEVE US? REFER TO YOUR HUMAN WARS IN YOUR HUMAN HISTORY BOOKS AND MAYBE YOU WILL LEARN SOMETHING.

When using **brute force**, first identify your target. Then gather any necessary weapons. Any missile, hammer, or explosive device will do. (We use whatever Rico has in his gullet.)

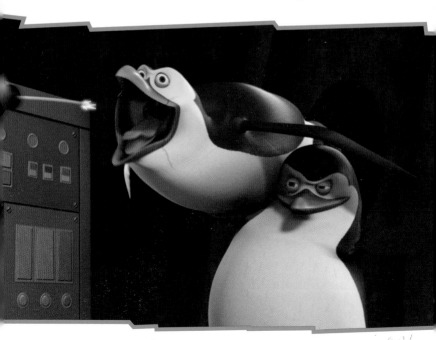

Remember to shoot first and ask questions **never**.

If you have **trouble** pulling the trigger, just think what would happen if you were attacked by an army of evil crabs and a one-eyed dolphin.

Sometimes, though, a problem can seem virtually indestructible. The kind of thing you can't destroy.

Like a brick wall.

Always proceed with caution when using big bombs, toxic chemicals, or your friend as a

PROJECTILE.

And remember: Problems aren't always made to be gotten through. Sometimes you have to go over or

around.

Sometimes, while in the process of trying to solve one problem, you may end up destroying something that had nothing to do with the problem at hand.

This is called **collateral damage**. As long as your problem is solved, you can chalk it up as lost for a cause. If you didn't solve your problem, you've just added more **fish** to the pile.

If you happen to create a bigger mess of the problem before solving it, it's perfectly acceptable to use the frustration you have about not destroying the thing you wanted to destroy to destroy other things—even if these new things are totally unrelated to your problem.

Sometimes you have to **make a mess to clean one up**.

With the frustration you were feeling out of your system, you'll have a clear head and can get back to tackling that original problem. **The brick wall.**

If you repeat this strategy enough times, you're sure to finally break through after all!

REMEMBER: IF AT FIRST YOU DON'T SUCCEED, DESTROY AND DESTROY AGAIN!

Chapter 9

LOGICALLY SPEAKING about LOGIC

All problems have **solutions**. It's a scientific fact. And logic is the scientist's tool to determine the correct solution to any crisis.

But even **logic has limitations**. True, it is extremely useful in a laboratory setting, where simple **cause** and **effect** can be measured in a controlled environment. In the real world, things are much more complicated. Even the simplest of life's problems is influenced by millions of factors.

How to **accurately measure** these factors and then **predict** the correct solution is one of the great mysteries of the universe. It has **confounded** scientists since I thought of the idea only moments ago.

For example, if you woke up one morning in a **guitar case** instead of your bed, you would think, *This could never happen! I must be dreaming.* Simple logic says this is impossible, yet it happened to me. (And was surprisingly comfortable.)

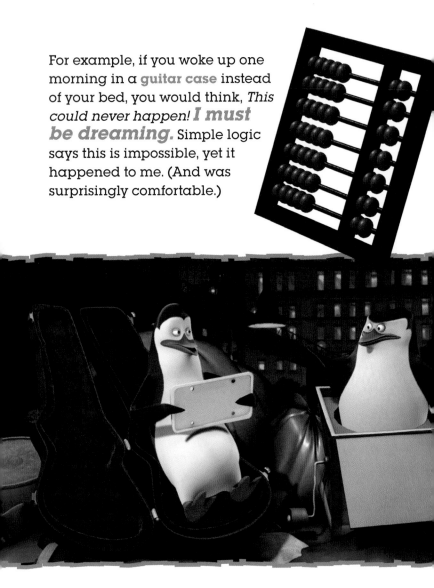

Logic would also say that **POPCORN** can't fall from the sky like rain.

But it has. And now I will check the local weather before planning my next movie night.

And even more **unlogical** would be a reptile opera!

But there was one. And it brought a **crocodile tear** to my eye.

My point is that life is so complex and is affected by so many factors, it takes a **master scientist** like me and a **supercomputer** to figure it all out. So to make this process easier for you, I set out to discover a single formula to determine the best solution to any crisis, no matter how bizarre, complicated, or **just plain weird** the problem may be.

Then the solution came to me in a flash while playing solitaire!

And like all great scientific breakthroughs, the answer was so **simple**. It was like it had been staring me in the face the whole time . . .

TaKe a Guess!

Seriously. Guess. After all, **anticipating** every possible solution, **determining** its statistical chances of success, and then mapping the algorithmic formulas of each possible outcome can take forever!

So **in an emergency**, shut your eyes, take a guess, and **hope for the best**!

SECTION III:

THERE IS NO END TO

FISH

Despite what you have read to this point, the bottom line is: **FiSH HaPPeNS**.

This can be scary for those who haven't been in hopeless situations regularly or recently. But there are ways to prepare for **the fishiest of fish**, like the **ZOMBie aPOCaLYPSe**, romantic breakups, and **red wine stains**.

Chapter 10

There's Action in RELAXIN'

When faced with a problem you can't solve, take a lesson from the great and wise Buddha and **do nothing**. In other words, relax!

To relax, lie back and **breathe deeply** until you drift away in blissful ignorance.

Then release all your tension as you **bask in the hopelessness** of the situation!

It helps to have onlookers for the most hopeless cases. Then you won't feel so alone.

Finally, close your eyes and let your mind turn to mush.

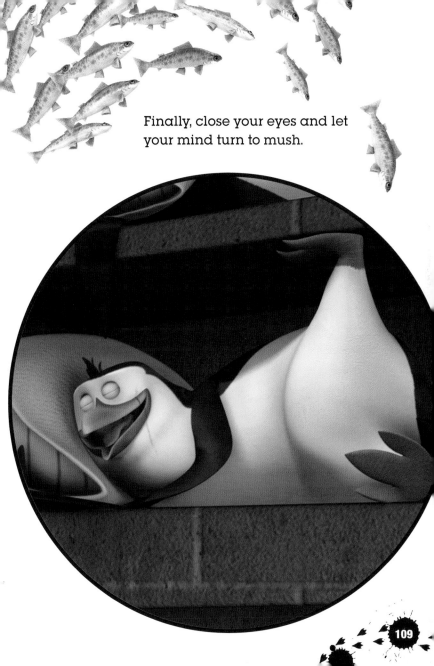

If after making several sincere attempts to do nothing about a problem you still find you can't achieve a relaxed state, find others who can help.

Everyone has problems they'd like to avoid, which is why relaxing is best done in a group. This way, no one feels **individually responsible** for not dealing with what's really going on. And you can always blame someone else if things get worse while you're doing nothing.

Have patience! Doing nothing about something takes **time**.

If you ignore problems long enough, they may resolve themselves on their own. Or become someone else's problem to deal with.

If after trying all of the above you still can't do nothing about a problem you can't solve, try staring into space with a **blank look** on your face.

Staring into space is almost as good as relaxing, with the added benefit of sending your friends a clear signal that says "**HEY, I NEED SOME HELP!**"

Chapter 11

PUT ONE Foot in Front of EVERYONE ELSE'S

When problems get to a critical level, it might be time to **run for your life**.

This is especially useful when you're being **chased** or when something is about to **blow up**.

You can easily simulate these large-scale disaster scenarios and others by playing video games. These virtual worlds are just like real life!*

You'll want to play these for at least **eighty hours a week** to be adequately prepared.

*EXCEPT THAT IF YOU DIE, YOU CAN JUST START OVER. UNLIKE REAL LIFE.

Whether you're actually running for your life or just for your virtual life, **timing is everything**. Running for your life too early can cause you to look like a coward.

Or lose points!

And running for your life **too late** will cause
you to be blown up or eaten.

GAME OVER!

The ideal time to run for your life is when
            , but not so close that you can't get away.

While running away, make sure to **run faster** than anyone else. This way, if the thing that's chasing you catches up, it will eat them before it gets to you.

Acrobatics can help you escape if there are walls to climb or villains to kick. The fancier the maneuvers, the more likely you are to survive.

Just be sure to **nail that landing** if you want those saving-your-own-butt bonus points!

And of course, aerial antics and flying **loopdy-loops** are surefire ways to increase your chances of escape.

Doing this will **WOW** onlookers and your gaming nerd friends as well as **save your life**.

Then, **if you survive**, you won't just be alive to tell a great story—you just might live on to virtual immortality by having someone make a video game based on your life!

Chapter 12

PANIC MAKES Perfect!

If a problem occurs and none of the previous strategies have worked, it's

Panic is the body's way of distracting you before something terrible and unavoidable happens.

Panic comes naturally to most. But if it doesn't come naturally to you, here are some easy steps to follow so when it's time to panic you don't feel left out.

Start by flailing your arms in the air. This says to all around you, "I have lost control of myself and am useless in this situation."

Next, let panic read clearly on your face. A **panicked look** is nearly universal and should be easy for all to identify. However, there is some variation due to personal style.

You'll want to accompany your flailing arms and panicked facial expression with a statement like,

"THE END IS NEAR!"

or **"NOOOOOOO!"**

If you can, **faint**. This will clearly indicate to all around that you are unable to respond to commands and have given yourself over to **full victim status**.

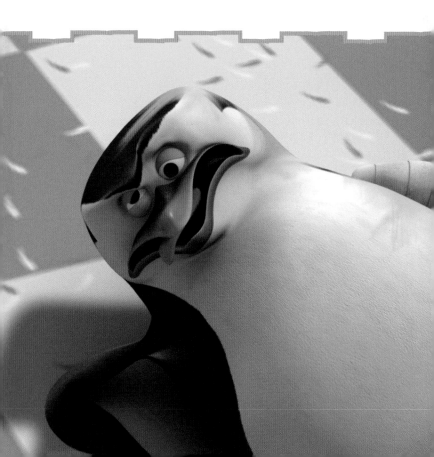

If possible, you'll want to **panic in large groups**, as many of these gestures seem ridiculous when performed alone.

Panicking will not only help pass the time before the inevitable occurs, but will also release you from any blame should you survive the incident at hand so you can simply say,

"I COULDN'T DO ANYTHING. I PANICKED."

keep It
POSITIVE

Hiiiiiiii!

It's me. I'm Mort! I get to tell you the last tip to solving your problems. I'm so excited! I like things that are hopeless, dangerous, or involve my doom.

Mostly because the word *doom* is fun to say.
D O O O O O O O O M. Wheeee!

But also because I only look at the bright side of any situation. You can, too, by remembering to **stay positive**.

Being positive all the time takes **practice**. For me, it took years to become good at it.

Mostly by dealing with a lot of bad situations that I couldn't control.

For example, if you've fallen off a high building, don't think of it as **falling**
   to
      your

        D O O O O O O O O O M.

Think of it as **learning to fly**, but only for a few seconds.

When I really have trouble thinking positively, though, I just focus on the things that I like most in the **whole**, **wide world**.

Like King Julien.

And King Julien's **feet**.

If you don't think King Julien's feet are the most marvelous things in the whole, wide world, that's okay. **I don't want to share** his feet with anyone, anyway. You can think of your own favorite things . . .

You see, it doesn't matter **how** you think positively, only that you **do it**!

I promise, if you start being positive, you'll have fewer problems than ever because you won't see all the

dooooooooooooooooooom

coming your way!

IN CONCLUSION

Well, there you have it.

FiSH HappeNs.

To all of us. At any time or place. There's nothing you can do to stop it. So you might as well **make the best of it**.

We hope you've found some **useful tips** in this book for **dealing with your problems**. We're sure you have, because we give good advice. Mostly because **we're smarter than you humans**, but also because we've dealt with **our fair share of fish**.

The next time something fishy happens to you:

Take a **DEEP** breath.

Then remember something **worse** is probably happening to **someone else**.

But always **be prepared** for the **unexpected**!

Keep your eyes open and **your nose up,** and you just might **smell that fish** before **it happens to you.**